Revolutionary Leadership

7 Steps to Be A Highly Effective Leader and Keep Your Best Talent

Michael Appiah

Copyright © Michael Appiah, 2018

The author reserves all the right to this book. They do not permit anyone to reproduce or transmit any part of this book through any means or form be it electronic or mechanical. No one also has the right to store the information herein in a retrieval system, neither do they have the right to photocopy, record copies, scan parts of this document, etc., without the proper written permission of the publisher or author.

Disclaimer

All the information in this book is to be used for informational and educational purposes only. The author will not account in any way for any results that stem from the use of the contents herein. While conscious and creative attempts have been made to ensure that all information provided herein is as accurate and useful as possible, the author is not legally bound to be responsible for any damage caused by the accuracy as well as use/misuse of this information.

ACKNOWLEDGMENTS

I thank God for giving me the vision to write this book. I appreciate my uncles Mr. Owusu Adarkwah and Mr. Michael Asomaning for the mentorship and guidance they have provided me since I was a little child. Many thanks to the youth and adults of the Toronto and Heritage Ghanaian Seventh-day Adventist Churches for the nurturing and support you've given to me for 25 plus years. Many thanks to Mr. John K. Baafi for encouraging me to pursue entrepreneurship and empowering me to utilize my skills to serve executives in the corporate sector. Eliezer Berefo, your relentless hard work, and inspiration to impact others positively are contagious. Godwin and Kevin, my best friends, the candor conversations we have had for so many years have challenged me to be a better person in all aspects of my life. My younger siblings: Nana Kofi Obeng, Abraham and Josephine, I hope and pray that I continue to be an inspiration to you. My older siblings: Samuel, Freda, and Kwabena, the successes you all have achieved in your professions are inspirational. I thank you so much for setting the bar for your little brother. My Parents: J. E. Appiah and Christiana Appiah, your diligence and sacrifice over the years are beyond amazing. Your parenting, guidance, and molding over the years have helped me to become a Christian and a person of high character.

Lastly, to my lovely wife, Marcelle, your unselfishness and unwavering support is fantastic. Your 'how can I help?' mentality is always appreciated even when I am stubborn and say, 'I don't need any help.'

FOREWORD

Through the years of knowing Michael, I have seen his mastery and demonstration of leadership skills in the most challenging situations. He possesses a unique ability to influence even the most challenging people amongst us in the leadership roles he's served in.

While watching "Billions," new favorite show of mine, it occurred to me that many organizations, especially those I have worked with, do not have a leadership coach. A performance coach is simply someone who can help you perform to a level better than your current best. Someone who won't settle for the dull and usual "just good enough." Essentially, someone that can shift their organization's paradigm to become a category market leader.

With more than seven years of consulting in the information security arena of the corporate world, working with the executive brass and employees, I have seen the need to empower leaders to bridge the gap between them and the employees, increase cohesion and create synergies that will ultimately produce an environment that fosters unity. This kind of work environment impacts the market share of the organization significantly.

What's remarkable is that many would think that such an enormous task should best go to a named brand firm, but Michael connects with people at a cellular level. He has the "you get me" factor, despite not being in the business sector.

In this book, *Revolutionary Leadership - 7 Steps To Be A Highly Effective Leader And Keep Your Best Talent,* you will not only learn seven steps to becoming a highly effective leader. The book will challenge you to be a revolutionary leader, especially in recent times where employee turnover has increased significantly in all parts of the world.

Start the journey by reading this book now.

~**J. K. Baafi**

Information Security Consultant

planBinfosec.com

Contents

ACKNOWLEDGMENTS 3

FOREWORD 5

INTRODUCTION 10

CHAPTER ONE 15

   Look at The Mirror 15

CHAPTER TWO 29

   Reinvent Yourself 29

CHAPTER THREE 43

   Diagnose Organizational Culture 43

      Types of Organizational Culture 48

      How to Change Organizational Culture 54

CHAPTER FOUR 58

   Be Emotionally Intelligent 58

      Key Elements of Emotional Intelligence 61

      Tools for Measuring Emotional Intelligence 64

      How to Build Emotional Intelligence 67

CHAPTER FIVE 72

   Create A Revolutionary Culture 72

CHAPTER SIX 85

    Be Innovative 85

        Characteristics of Innovative leaders 90

        How to Become Innovative 94

CHAPTER SEVEN 98

    Keep Growing 98

        Benefits of Commitment to Leadership Growth 101

        Tips for Leadership Growth 103

CONCLUSION 110

About the Author 111

INTRODUCTION

One of the most critical issues executives face as they compete for human resources in a tight economy is employee retention. Aside from the costs of employee turnover that are increasingly high (sometimes almost 2.5 times more than the basic salary), there are other adverse effects of low employee retention like decreased engagement, lowered productivity, among others.

At no time in history has more people quit their jobs in the United States than we have today. Data from the U. S. Labor Department revealed that job openings in the U. S. hit a new peak of 6.94m in July 2018 and the highest number of workers since 2001 quit their positions. Data from the U. S. Bureau of Labor Statistics has it that about three million employees quit their jobs each month voluntarily in the U. S. A study conducted by BambooHR reported that of the over 1000 workers sampled, nearly a third of term had left their jobs within the first six months of being hired. Most of the participants left their jobs because of a less-than-excellent boss, lack of clear delineation of duties and expectations, or poor relationship with other team members.

According to a study conducted by LinkedIn (2018), France has 21% employee turnover, United Kingdom has about 17.6% employee turnover, Australia has about 17.5% employee turnover, while Canada has about 16% employee turnover. These figures show that all around the world, there is high level of employee turnover.

It is becoming more glaring and worthier of note to executives and managers that it takes much more than increased pay to increase their capacity for employee retention. Employees don't continue to give their best to the company only because they are paid well. The quality of leadership in the organization is a significant factor that determines whether employees will decide to stay with a firm or not.

Corporate culture has changed significantly around the world, and it influences the commitment of employees to an organization. Variables such as the involvement of employees in decision-making, adaptability of the management to changing economic realities, nature of communication, among others contribute to the employee retention capacity of an organization. Only companies that have managers who can be aware of these changes and adjust to them will win the hearts of talented and dedicated employees and also retain them.

Some people believe that all it takes to be a good manager is common sense. If this were true, good managers would be everywhere and the rate of employee turnover will not be as high as it is. It will be difficult for managers who subscribe to the "common sense" view of management to seek for the required knowledge and exert the necessary effort in leading their teams.

This book will provide information for leaders who want to be revolutionary. I will take you through 7 steps that will make you the kind of leader that every employee desire. You will learn how to retain the commitment and zeal of your followers and achieve your organizational goals faster.

Let's jump right in.

CHAPTER ONE

LOOK AT THE MIRROR

"The most fundamental aggression to ourselves, the most fundamental harm we can do to ourselves, is to remain ignorant by not having the courage and the respect to look at ourselves honestly and gently."

~ Pema Chodron

David was a young shepherd who was only taking care of the sheep of his father. One day, his father sent him to give some welfare packages to his brothers who were on the war front. He got there and heard a giant defaming the name of God. He was told how that everyone including the king was afraid of confronting the giant. David offered to fight with the giant, and with his shepherd's sling and stone, he defeated Goliath, the giant.

David, subsequently, rose to become an influential leader in Israel. However, he lost the sense of the man he was, took the wife of one of his trusted soldiers who was on the battlefield, and organized the death of the soldier. It took the prophet Nathan (a trusted advisor) to bring him to that point of self-assessment, where he reflected on what had happened and saw the gravity of the offense he had committed. Nathan had to tell David the story of a corrupt leader, before David came back to his senses and then Nathan confronted him with the truth by saying 'it is you.'

Just like David was unaware of how much less a great leader he was at this point; many executives and managers are unaware of how much they had become less of great people than they were before they became leaders. To worsen the case, some of us executives and managers have silenced every 'Nathan' that could bring us to that point of self-assessment. We believe that what we are doing has to be right. We don't have the time to look into the mirror and reflect on the weaknesses, strengths, and consequences of our leadership styles.

According to Michelle Roccia, the Executive Vice President of Employee Engagement at Winter Wyman, "self-assessment is an essential part of performance evaluation, because it's an opportunity for you to assess your achievements." If we don't spare some time to answer some hard-hitting questions about our performance as leaders objectively, we will never see the need to challenge ourselves to get better.

Self-assessment is the process through which performance and behavioral evaluation are conducted, with a view to determining necessary improvements for better leadership experience. When we practice self-assessment, we will uncover our areas of weakness and strength. We will know exactly how far we are from achieving personal and organizational goals.

There are several advantages of engaging in self-assessment. Some of them are discussed below.

- **Motivation:** when we undergo self-assessment, we track our progress in leadership performance. Being abreast of these achievements can serve as a source of motivation for the leader when things are tough. One reason why many of us give up is that we forget too soon how we have improved and become better over time; we refuse to acknowledge the progress we have made in more difficult situations than we are now. But if we pay attention to self-assessment, we will always be motivated to become better.

- **Self-awareness:** this is fundamental to effective leadership. Self-awareness involves having adequate knowledge of your strengths, weaknesses, values, desires, beliefs, emotions, personality, and character. No one that is not self-aware can be a revolutionary leader. Critical to self-awareness is self-assessment. When leaders carry out self-assessment, they can know their professional and personal identities, and this can inform the way they go about leadership for optimal performance.

- **Faster achievement of set goals:** When leaders carry out self-assessment, they can determine how they are faring concerning relationship with their followers. Once they have established this, they know what to improve on. The relationship between a leader and the followers can be a significant determinant of the zeal and dedication that those followers will commit to their work, and this can make all the difference between the achievement or non-achievement of set goals.

- **Increase in employee retention:** The process of self-assessment also involves getting honest feedback from people around who are trusted to tell the truth. When leaders do this, they will know what their employees feel about their style of leadership, approach to decision making, among other things. With this knowledge, they can seek improvement where necessary, and this will make the employees more comfortable working with such leaders. When employees know that their leader is willing to listen to them and make corrections even to his or her leadership style, they tend to love the leader more and prefer to remain in the organization.

From the preceding, it is evident that if we leaders don't pay attention to self-assessment, we will be missing out on a very crucial foundation for self-development and leadership fulfillment. Let me tell you my story.

Several years ago, I was a member of a youth leadership team. My leader was pretty much impressed by my contributions to the team that he nominated me as his successor. It did happen; I became the next leader after him. When I was made the leader, I vowed to myself that I would be different than my predecessor by ensuring that I encourage my team members to participate more in the decision-making process and to utilize their skills. However, as months passed by, I noticed that I could not live up to my vow as it had become challenging to engage my team members. I had to complete about 90% of all projects by myself. As expected, I got frustrated with the team and sent messages of disappointment to them because of their low level of involvement with the team.

This went on for a while, and one day I decided to get feedback from my team members. They opened up to me that I was too impatient and did not involve members of the team to lead projects frequently. This opened me up to the idea of self-assessment. I took some personality tests to understand myself better and where I can improve upon myself to better lead my team. The result was fantastic. My team members became more involved with the team, we completed our projects together and faster, they were happy, and I was delighted.

Several personality tests can be taken by leaders to help them 'look in the mirror,' some of them are discussed below.

- **DISC Assessment:** DISC refers to the behavior types that are assessed by this test. They are dominance, influence, steadiness, and compliance. This tool provides self-assessment of the impact of natural tendencies on the way leaders receive, process and deliver information. It is a widely used tool for self-assessment because it is relatively inexpensive, simple, easy to comprehend, and can be adapted to varying circumstances.

- **Myers Briggs Type Indicator:** This test is used to measure psychological preferences in the perception of the world by leaders, processing of information and decision-making. By taking this test, a leader can identify the personality types and how it affects the way both the leader and the team members think and communicate. It is relatively difficult to administer, but it provides a great deal of insight into your personality.

- **Multi-Source Assessment:** This test helps a leader to know what the team members, colleagues, and superiors think about his or her leadership performance and general behavior. This information can help a leader to identify the gap between the desired outcome and the real outcome of the decisions of that leader. This test is also called the 360-degree feedback.

- **The Strength-Finders:** this test helps leaders to achieve their set goals by helping them to identify, comprehend and maximally utilize their exclusive combination of skills, knowledge, and talents. In other words, the Strength-Finders test help leaders to become aware of their strengths. This test helps to identify leaders' top 5 strengths out of 34 possible strengths. The test is pivoted by a modern philosophical thought that says to focus more on your strengths for more happiness and better productivity.

- **John Maxwell Leadership Assessment:** This test is based on the five levels of leadership as postulated by John C. Maxwell. The test measures 64 characteristics that make leaders revolutionary. Leaders are assessed along position (trustworthiness and commitment), permission (relational abilities and interpersonal skills), production (achievement of personal and professional goals), people development (reproducing and developing leadership skills in others), and pinnacle (awareness of both self and others).

There are specific tips that I will like you to take note of as you seek to undergo self-assessment.

- **Listen more, talk less:** Many leaders know how to speak, but don't know how to listen. Listening is not all about being physically in a place and hearing the words that a person is saying; it is more about being ready to hear the speaker out without preconceived bias, asking questions to be sure you comprehend what the person has said and acting on what was said. So, as leaders who want to benefit from self-assessment, you must listen more than you talk.

- **Don't avoid difficult conversations:** While taking on self-assessment, you may need to have some difficult conversations with your team members; sometimes, an honest assessment of something that had happened in the past. However, you need to know what conversations to let go off and which to have. Determine the impact of the results of the discussion on your business or team members before you decide to have that conversation.

- **Admit mistakes and apologize:** Revolutionary leaders are not afraid to apologize when they discover that they have made mistakes. When apologizing, however, don't just say 'I am sorry.' Be specific about what you are sorry about and let the other party(s) know that you are committed to avoiding such next time.

- **Keep communication with your team members open:** Self-assessment should not be a once-in-a-lifetime thing. As revolutionary leaders, we must create platforms by which our team members can assess us easily and communicate our shortcomings to us. We should be deliberate about this.

In conclusion, self-assessment helps in bringing reforms to a leader's lifestyle, contributes to a better comprehension of your team members and helps to achieve set personal and professional goals. You should take a test today!

CHAPTER TWO

REINVENT YOURSELF

"Success is not final, failure is not fatal: it is the courage to continue that counts."

~Winston Churchill

Abraham Lincoln was born in rural Kentucky and grew up without a silver spoon in his mouth. His father was not educated and didn't have the ambition to be, his mother taught him to read and write, but she died when he was only nine. He was subsequently lent out to farmers who needed workers. However, Lincoln did not allow the challenges he experienced while growing up to hinder him from being successful; he reinvented himself.

Lincoln, with immense passion and determination, used literature to rebuild his mind to cope with the demands of being successful. He read the works of Shakespeare and Aesop so well that he could recite several passages off-hand. He learned English grammar, trigonometry and geometry by himself. At that time, young men who were learning law were attached to practicing lawyers, but Lincoln studied by himself. He borrowed law books and read them over and over again until he comprehended them thoroughly.

Lincoln rose from a poor rural boy to the President of the United States who demonstrated exceptional leadership skills. It is said that what Abraham Lincoln knew about leadership about 150 years ago is still exceptional knowledge today. Shortly after becoming the U. S. president, he appointed the three men he defeated to his cabinet. This is what is popularly referred to as the team of rivals. Lincoln did not start his life as an extraordinary leader, but along the way, he reinvented himself. He made mistakes, learned from his mistakes, never gave up, grew until he became a revolutionary leader.

Kristen Haded, the founder and CEO of Student Maid (a cleaning company that hires student), started the company shortly after she graduated from College at 21. While she was in college, at 19, she wanted to purchase a pair of jeans, and so, she put an ad on craigslist that she was willing to clean a house. The person who answered the ad taught her how to clean a house and hired her again every single week.

When she finished college, she got a contract that she could not complete by herself, she needed to hire a team of people to do the work with her, and this is where the company started from. This was the point where she was exposed to leadership, but she failed; about seventy-five percent of her team members resigned in one day. This was the moment that compelled her to learn about leadership and how to build strong teams. The result was that she became a more effective leader with a better team, and now, she teaches others how to lead.

I have shared the story of these two successful leaders with you to say to you that irrespective of the condition in your firm at the moment, you can rise above it. You can build a firm that will become a reference point for success to all other firms. Your team can be strong; your team members can be happy, and desirous to stay with your firm for a longer time. What you need is to reinvent yourself.

Life is like a marathon race. If you must possess the ability to stay on top of challenges that you experience in life, you must continually evolve with time. The process of reinvention is essential, mainly if you are handling a leadership role. There is arguably no world leader who doesn't reinvent himself or herself continually. As leaders reinvent themselves, they can prepare their teams to tackle the challenges that come with a change in the physical, social and economic conditions of the State.

So, you may ask, 'how do I know it's time to reinvent myself?'

Discussed below are clear signs that a leader needs reinvention.

- **Ongoing Conflicts within your team:** Perhaps, you have managed your team well for a period, but suddenly conflicts started becoming the order of the day. You settle one today; you have another tomorrow. This is a clear sign that you, the leader, needs reinvention. It could also be that there is always unresolvable conflict concerning a topic, such that whenever the issue comes up, the conflict also comes up; you, the leader needs to reinvent yourself. Furthermore, if you are always having a face-off with one of your team members, you, as a leader, need to reinvent yourself.
- **Not getting desired results:** If your team has always beat the deadline, achieved your set goals, but suddenly, the team seems not to be beating the deadlines any longer, the goals are not met any longer, it is a clear sign that the leader needs reinvention.

- **Team members are disengaged:** Usually, when leaders led well, team members will be excited about what they are doing. They will turn up for meetings early; they will seldom give excuses not to beat deadlines. However, when the team members are disengaged from the goals of the team when they no longer show the same passion and commitment to the team, it is an indication that the leader needs reinvention.
- **The leadership thrill is gone:** If you as the leader is less passionate about the team, or the idea to take on the next project seems less attractive to you, then you need to reinvent yourself. When you cannot find good reasons to lead anymore, you no longer enjoy your leadership, you need to reinvent yourself.

Reinventing yourself as a leader will help to keep you in the leadership game, retain your positivity, rise above challenges, redefine who you are, and ensure you don't get bored.

I Surmise that the question on your mind is so, 'how do I reinvent myself?' Discussed below are trusted and proven steps to reinventing yourself as a leader.

- **Objectively analyze the current situation:** Before you can reinvent yourself, you must know what needs reinvention. To understand this, you must examine the case you are in at the moment. You can achieve this by thinking in retrospect about what you have been doing in times past that you no longer do, or what you were not doing that you have started to do. You should also engage your team members; humbly ask what their opinion is about your leadership. You can assess the current situation along the following lines of thought:

Style and approach: when your leadership style is outdated, your team members will not respond to you as they always do in time past. They will no longer be willing to follow your leadership because you have stopped growing. You should assess yourself and see if it is your leadership style and approach that is the cause of the problem.

Entitlement: when you act in ways that make your team members feel that they owe you something, they see you as being power hungry, and they will stop responding to your leadership as expected. You should find out if you are making your team members have that feeling that they are entitled to you.

Disrespect: when you make your team-members feel less human than they are by disregarding and disrespecting them, you will lose their followership. Some traditional leaders think that by assuming the position of leadership, they now have the power to mistreat others, but this makes them lose their team members. So, also, find out whether your team members are feeling disrespected by the way you relate with them or they think you are rude.

Selfishness: if your followers think that you are selfish (only concerned about your achievement as a leader), they will lose the thrill to commit themselves to your leadership. So, you need to find out whether you are selfish, or your team members think you are selfish.

Disorganization: when you are not clear as to what your goals and objectives are, and your team members are not sure what their duties and expectations are, they will not commit themselves to your leadership anymore. They will be searching for the next available opportunity to leave. You should assess yourself to know if disorganization is the reason for the situation you are in at the moment.

Lack of Vision: when you lack vision, you set unrealistic goals. You will never appreciate the work your team members have done; your mind will always be on what they are yet to accomplish. When this happens, the team members will lose interest in your leadership. This could also be a reason why you are in the situation you are currently.

When you have assessed yourself along these lines, you will know where the problem lies. Don't forget to involve your team members in the assessment.

Learn: as soon as you discover the problem that has brought you the results that you don't desire, you need to start learning how to fix the problem. You can learn by reading books on leadership, listening to podcasts, attending leadership conferences, going to leadership schools, among others. You should create time for leadership development as part of your daily schedule. You should have an hour or two every day which you dedicate to developing your leadership capabilities. Also, learn by observing the current trends in the leadership world; find out how other leaders are coping with their team members. Ask questions, be humble.

Implement: Many leaders have stuff on their heads that could turn their organizations around for the better but lack the skills to implement them. To achieve proper implementation of things you have learned, discuss with your team members. Never relegate them to the background. Make them aware of what you have discovered, what you have learned and ask them for their thoughts on the implementation. This will make them feel respected, and in turn, they will be more committed to the team.

As a leader, you don't have to wait till things are bad before you reinvent yourself, reinvention should be an ongoing thing for a leader who wants to be revolutionary. Here are some tips that could help you to keep reinventing yourself.

- Never make excuses for your failures
- Never play the blame game
- Always listen to your team members
- Create a platform or system by which your team members can freely express their minds to you

- Keep learning – devote time to leadership development every day
- Don't allow past failures to weigh you down – be optimistic
- See every challenge as an opportunity to get better
- Get leadership coaching
- Network with other leaders.

Reinventing yourself is the way to go to become a revolutionary leader.

CHAPTER THREE

DIAGNOSE ORGANIZATIONAL CULTURE

"The way I think about culture is that modern humans have radically changed the way that they work and the way that they live. Companies need to change the way they manage and lead to match the way that modern humans actually work and live."

~Brian Halligan (CEO, HubSpot)

Organizational culture is the aggregation of beliefs, values, philosophies, and behaviors that influence both the emotional and social environment of a workplace. Corporate culture is the subtle, impalpable, inner layer of an organization that guides thought processes and determine the outer layer (behavior, processes, structure, among others) of the organization. When externals go wrong in an organization, it is essential that the leader finds out if the problem comes from the culture of the organization. Aside from when things go wrong, leaders can diagnose and improve the culture of an organization to enhance the performance of the firm concerning realizing their set goals and desires.

The UK Power Networks (UKPN) was formed in 2011 from the acquisition of 3 electricity networks in London by Cheung Kong Infrastructure Holdings (CKI), and it is expected to deliver electricity to about 20 million people, which is about a quarter of Britain's population. The CEO, Basil Scarsella shaped the culture of the new company to help achieve the goal of delivering a reliable first-class network that customers are satisfied with, cost-efficient and safe.

The effect of the culture change is evident in the awards received by the company. For example, in 2013, the company has won the Best Business Award for Best Customer Focus; in 2014, the company received an award for the way the workforce is led and developed consistently for improved service.

According to Scarsella, the best thing experienced by the company is a significant improvement in performance in all areas including engagement from employees, the reliability of the network, customer satisfaction, among others. Scarsella believes that the achievement of these feats is made possible by the work that was done in putting up the culture and the commitment of both the management team and employees to sustaining that culture.

Organizational culture is everything about a company. It shows in the way the company business is conducted, and how employees and customers are treated. It is also expressed in the extent to which employees are allowed to participate in the decision-making process, develop new ideas and show their ingenuity. Company culture is what determines how information and power flow within the firm, and ultimately, the commitment of the employees towards the collective goals and objectives of the firm. Invariably, organizational culture can determine what the rate of employee turnover will be for a firm. If the culture is excellent, employee turnover will be low, if the culture is terrible, employee turnover will be high.

Types of Organizational Culture

Some of the different types of organizational culture are discussed below.

- **Clan Culture:** This type of culture emphasizes friendliness. Both the employers and the employees have a lot in common. Usually, the employees see the leaders and executives as father figures and mentors. Loyalty and tradition hold the organization together. Employees are substantially involved in the decision-making process of the organization. Great emphasis is laid on the development of human resources. Organization success is defined by how much the needs of the clients are met and how much the employees are catered for.
- **Adhocracy Culture:** this culture prioritizes innovation above all else. Success is

defined by the creation of new products and services. Both leaders and employees are encouraged to take risks and innovate. The binding factor in the organization is innovation and experimentation. What leaders seek to promote among employees is taking the initiative individually and freedom of expression of such initiative.

- **Market Culture:** The organizations that operate this kind of culture focus on getting things done and finishing assigned work. Leaders and executives work diligently to produce, but they see themselves as rivals. Therefore, they have high expectations for their employees, and they are usually hard on them. The binding cord of the organization is the emphasis on winning. Success is defined by how much the organization penetrates the market.

Competition is the fundamental organization style.

- **Hierarchy Culture:** This type of culture emphasizes structure and formal procedures. All activities are carried out strictly by following laid down procedures. There is no opportunity for creativity and innovation. Leaders pride themselves in the fact that everyone functions strictly by rules and regulations. Policies and formal rules hold the organization together. Success is defined by how much an employee can keep to the rules and regulations of the organization.

Organizational culture determines how employees perceive the organization. It determines whether the employees want to stay or go. When leaders see the need to diagnose corporate culture, there are specific components of the culture that needs to be studied, some of them are discussed below.

- **Communication:** This is a very vital component of organizational culture. It relates to the way information is circulated within the organization. It involves both formal communications like the circulation of a newsletter and informal communication like the discussions that go on in the break room. If the communication within an organization is faulty, employees will not be satisfied with the organization, and they will want to leave. However, if the communication lines are great, the employees will be committed to the organization. So, as a leader, when you decide to diagnose your organizational culture, start with the communication within the organization. Both communication between leaders, leaders to employees and employees to customers.

- **Behavioral Rules:** They may be unwritten codes, but they define how individuals within an organization interact with each other. They also influence how work is done in an organization. Leaders should also assess these rules when they diagnose organizational culture.

- **Rewards and Recognition:** Usually, the skills, behavior, and pattern of getting work done that are rewarded and recognized within an organization are on the one hand a result of organizational culture, on the other hand, they form the organizational culture. The most important things to the organization are reflected in the reward and recognition system of the organization.

- **Valued skills:** The leader who wants to assess the organizational culture should asses what skills are most important to the organization. This can be known by considering the skills that are most prominent in senior leaders. Skills that are used to judge qualification for promotion should also be considered.
- **Leadership style:** Organizational culture can determine the leadership styles of executives within the organization and this will in turn influence how employees feel about the organization. Leaders within an organization may subscribe to the autocratic style of leadership or democratic style, among others. Changing the leadership style can make all the needed difference in employees' attitude to the organization.

Although some people believe that organizational culture cannot be changed, it is essential for you, as a leader reading this book to believe that it can be changed. If you follow the steps below, you will know what is wrong with your organizational culture, and you will be able to change it in a way that both you and your employees will be happy.

How to Change Organizational Culture

- **Evaluate your current culture and performance:** In the previous section, I showed you components of organizational culture. The first step to changing your corporate culture is to know what is obtainable at the moment. Identify your performance priorities, organizational strengths, communication pattern, and leadership style. Find out which of these is empowering the organization to reach its maximum potential and which of them is serving as a limiting factor.

- **Involve your employees:** Leaders who are humble enough to ask questions often make more progress than those who think they know it all. In addition to your discoveries by taking the first step, ask your employees what they think about the organizational culture; how does it affect them and what areas do they feel needs improvement.
- **Set SMART goals:** After going through the first two steps, you must have identified critical areas of your organizational culture that is responsible for the lack of interest of employees in the organization. With the help of your employees, set SMART goals to change those faulty components of your organizational culture. SMART goals are specific, measurable, attainable, realistic and time-bound.

- **Model acceptable behavior:** Now that you have defined the goals to be achieved in changing your organizational culture, you, the leader, must begin to walk the talk. Let the change start with you. Even though you involved your team in the change process, and you have communicated what they need to know, they will still look to you to display your expectations. This is most important during a culture change. If you are not willing to change, you cannot expect your employees to improve.
- **Create accountability platforms:** Accountability is one of the significant ways by which leaders can help their employees to follow the change in culture. To ensure accountability, employees must have detailed job descriptions with explicitly defined measures. This will make them know how you want to begin to describe success. They must

understand the deliverables in the new culture and when each is due.

- **Bring the new culture home:** By this, I mean that you make the new culture personal to your employees. Let them develop personal words or sentences that communicates the change you want to make. Ask them to discuss how this new change will motivate them to achieve more both for themselves and the organization.

Without a great organizational culture, no organization can be significant. There is nothing exceptional about an organization except its culture. Diagnose your organizational culture today and see the tremendous amount of change that can take place within your employees.

CHAPTER FOUR

BE EMOTIONALLY INTELLIGENT

"When dealing with people, remember you are not dealing with creatures of logic, but with creatures of emotion."

~Dale Carnegie

Jeff Bezos, the CEO of Amazon is an example of a leader with high emotional intelligence. Sometimes in 2015, Amazon was ranked the 464th firm with the lowest employee turnover out of the Fortune 500 companies by Payscale. Although the median tenure was 12 months, Amazon has been hiring employees at an astounding rate. However, with this level of success, some people have criticized Amazon fulfillment centers for difficult working conditions. Bezos responded by saying that "these anecdotes of callous management practices don't describe the Amazon I know or the caring Amazonians I work with every day. But if you know of any stories like those reported, I want you to escalate to HR. You can also email me directly at jeff@amazon.com. Even if it is rare or isolated, our tolerance for any such lack of empathy needs to be zero." Considering this response by Bezos, we cannot ascertain how angered he may have been, but we can say for sure that this response demonstrates emotional maturity and intelligence. He left no stone unturned to encourage empathy, self-confidence, communication, among others.

Emotional intelligence is the ability of a person to manage both personal emotions and those of others. Going by this definition, emotional intelligence has two parts: one is controlling your feelings, the other is managing the feelings of others. Emotional intelligence is a critical skill for leaders who want to be revolutionary. Emotional intelligence is usually an aggregation of psychological awareness (the ability to determine your emotion), the capacity to use identified emotions to solve problems, and the ability to cheer up or calm down others as the case may require.

There are five key elements of emotional intelligence, which, if managed well, will increase your emotional intelligence as a leader. Let's consider them in details.

Key Elements of Emotional Intelligence

- **Self-Awareness:** to be self-aware is to be conscious of who you are and how you feel at every given point. If you are self-aware, you will know how your actions which are based on your emotions affect the people you work with. For a leader, self-awareness includes a clear, and precise knowledge of your strengths and weaknesses, which will help you to be humble. Several ways exist by which you can improve your self-awareness; some of them are to keep journals, ask questions from people you work with, identify the triggers of bad emotions, slow down to determine the reason you are feeling bad emotions before reacting to them, among others.

- **Self-Regulation:** This is an essential component of emotional intelligence that relates to how leaders control themselves when they feel bad emotions. If you can regulate yourself to avoid verbal bout on others, hasty decisions, and compromising your values, then your emotional intelligence is high. The main thing about self-regulation is staying in control of your actions, words, and reactions at all times. You can increase your ability for self-regulation by being aware of your values, holding yourself accountable for your actions, words, and responses, and practicing calmness.

- **Motivation:** The ability to consistently work towards the achievement of your set goals in the face of challenges and the capacity to inspire others to keep pursuing personal or common set goals while maintaining high standards for their quality of work are components of emotional intelligence. You can improve your level of motivation by re-assessing why you are doing what you are doing, setting smart goals and objectives, encouraging yourself by past victories, among others.

- **Empathy** is the ability to put yourself in someone else's condition. Empathetic leaders listen to their followers and give constructive feedback to them. They also challenge the followers who are not acting reasonably and help their followers to improve. By being empathic, leaders can earn respect and loyalty of their followers. As a leader, you can increase your empathy level by paying attention to body language of your followers, responding to their feelings, listening to them, among others.

- **Social skills:** leaders with high emotional intelligence are excellent communicators. They know how to get their people to key into and be excited about the goals of the organization. Social skills help leaders to resolve conflicts and manage change. They don't only give instructions to their followers; they participate in the work themselves. You can improve your social skills by learning conflict resolution, developing your communication skills, and learning to praise others.

There are several tools for measuring the emotional intelligence of an individual. They are discussed below.

Tools for Measuring Emotional Intelligence

- **Ability Tools:** Individuals who use the ability tools to measure their emotional intelligence test themselves against right answers determined by Emotional intelligence practitioners. To use the ability tools effectively, you need to establish aforehand the context where you want to apply emotional intelligence; this will inform the tasks you will perform in the assessment. There are ability tools to assess leadership, well-being, among others, you should pre-determine which you want to use. The major criticism against the use of ability tools in measuring emotional intelligence is that the fact that someone knows the right behavior in an emotional situation does not mean the person will eventually demonstrate that proper behavior. One of the instruments used in this category is the Mayer-Salovey-Caruso Emotional Intelligence Test (MSCEIT).

- **Trait Tools:** These tools rely on personal information to determine a person's emotional intelligence, in other words, the assessment is primarily based on self-report. The criticism against using these tools to measure emotional intelligence is that many people believe that self-report is not dependable to gauge how someone would react to an emotional situation. One of the instruments used in this category is the Schutte Self Report Emotional Intelligence Test.

- **Mixed Tools:** here, several qualities of emotional intelligence are measured together. For example, emotion triggers like knowledge and understanding, empathy, competencies, attitudes, traits and other inspirational qualities are weighed together to give the emotional intelligence of the subject. It is almost impossible to measure all these qualities with a single instrument; therefore, usually, several instruments are used while measuring emotional intelligence using mixed tools. In the end, emotional intelligence is described as a percentage of the instruments used. The criticism against this model is that there is a tendency to classify any behavior as intelligence.

I suppose that you will be happy to know that emotional intelligence can be learned. You can increase the level of your emotional intelligence. Discussed below are strategies that will help you improve your emotional intelligence.

How to Build Emotional Intelligence

- **Observe:** Much of what you do to improve your emotional intelligence is to observe. You will need to observe how you react to people when you feel certain emotions, identify your weaknesses and strengths, get to know how your actions, words, and reactions affect others. Also, you must determine the places, people and circumstances that make you feel bad emotions. This step is critical to developing emotional intelligence.

- **Learn:** after you have discovered your triggers of bad emotions, you must learn how to avoid them. You must learn to avoid the people, places, and situations that make you feel bad emotions. You must also learn to be calm, to refuse to speak until you have reasonably concluded that it is better to talk. Learn to build a good rapport with the people you are working with. Learn to be empathic.

- **Take responsibility:** in your journey to developing emotional intelligence, it is certain that you will mess up at some points. It is good that you take responsibility for your actions, words, and reactions. When you hurt someone's feelings, don't overlook it or avoid them, be deliberate about rendering an apology. Let them know you are sorry for what has happened and that you are willing to do everything possible within your power to make sure such doesn't happen in the future.

- **Be happy:** It is practically impossible to feel good and bad emotions at the same time. Therefore, if you spend more time with people that make you happy, doing things that make you happy and being in places that make you happy, you have reduced the amount of time left to feel bad emotions. It is not possible to completely avoid bad feelings, but you can drastically reduce the periods you feel bad emotions.

- **Always consider others:** Before you act or react to any lousy emotion you are feeling, take some time to think about how the recipient of the action or reaction will feel. Never allow the desire to seek revenge cloud your mind.

- **Communicate:** To develop emotional intelligence, you must be willing to communicate. Communication is not only in speaking, but it is also in listening. You cannot manage another person's emotions if you don't listen to them. So, take time out to listen to your team members. Create a system by which your team members can talk to you freely. Also, learn to choose your words carefully, and know when to keep quiet.

- **Praise others:** When any of your team members does something good, don't overlook it, applaud them. Applause for a job well done has a way of motivating an individual to do more.

- **Encourage your team members to take Emotional Intelligence Tests:** As a leader, one of your duties is to make sure your team members improve in all fronts. Therefore, part of the ways to improve your emotional intelligence, the part of managing their emotions is to motivate them to take tests that will help them know what level they are concerning emotional intelligence and how to improve.

By following the steps discussed above, you will be able to develop your emotional intelligence, and you will be a better leader.

CHAPTER FIVE

CREATE A REVOLUTIONARY CULTURE

"You have to be a place that's more than a paycheck for people."

~Rick Federico

There is one challenge that is common to organizations; it is a problem of getting several individuals with different backgrounds, training, mindset and thought processes to combine into a single entity. In other words, the challenge of making all employees key into the culture, goal, and objectives of a firm is enormous. However,

Gregg Popovich of the San Antonio Spurs has been able to solve this problem to a large extent in the organization. Let's find out how.

Over the past two decades, the San Antonio Spurs have won 5 championships. They have become America's most successful sports franchise with a 713 winning percentage and 20 successive winning seasons. The secret to their winning culture is in their practice. Gregg Popovich, the coach of San Antonio Spurs, is known for his blunt, intense leadership style.

According to Daniel Coyle, when he visited the team, Popovich was not shouting at any of the team members. He was only walking around, talking to his players laughing with them and speaking to them in their languages. Popovich connected with a player by moving very close to him that their noses would almost touch each other. When a former player showed up,

Popovich's face beamed up lightly, they talked for a few minutes and parted.

According to the assistant coach Chip Engelland, "a lot of coaches can yell or be nice, but what Pop does is different, he delivers two things over and over: he'll tell you the truth, with no BS, and then he'll love you to death." This means that aside from correcting his team, Pop also loved them, and this is the secret for their victory. He connected with the team and made sure they also connected with each other; he demonstrated that he cared about them, and yet he was disciplined and instilled discipline in the organization.

After careful analysis of the current culture in your organization and comprehending the team members' personalities through tests, you must create a revolutionary culture with a mixture of leadership styles that will work best to motivate individuals to become better and achieve success.

Different leadership styles exist that a leader could employ in the workplace; some of the prominent ones are discussed below.

- **Autocratic Leadership:** Leaders who use this style wield a lot of power over the people working with them. The team members are not involved in decision-making even if their suggestion would have made the decision better. The organization functions on instructions, you have to obey the standing order. When leaders become autocratic, decisions are made on time and work is done more effectively. However, most people don't want to be treated this way. Autocratic leadership results in high employee turnover and absenteeism. The military uses the authoritarian leadership style, because of the nature of their assignment. Also, autocratic leadership can be useful for unskilled jobs, where the benefit of control outweighs the disadvantages of the leadership style.

- **Bureaucratic Leadership:** Leaders who use this style work strictly by rules and regulations, and they ensure that all employees work with procedures. This style is appropriate for jobs where employees have to follow particular rules to be safe, such that disobeying one rule can lead to loss of body part. For example, those who work with heavy and dangerous types of machinery, chemicals or those who have to climb to dangerous heights. It could also be useful in jobs that involve large amounts of money. If the employees do routine tasks, bureaucratic leadership style could be an efficient style that a leader could employ. However, bureaucratic leadership will fail when applied to jobs that require creativity and flexibility. Team members could feel that they cannot give their optimum and so, the employee turnover will be high.

- **Charismatic Leadership:** Charismatic leaders are excellent at motivating their team to make progress and achieve set goals. They have the unique ability to make team members excited about and committed to what they do. However, charismatic leaders focus more on themselves; they always believe in their skills and are usually incorrigible. This attitude can ruin the team and the organization. Also, the employees of charismatic leaders will never think that they can do anything worthwhile without the presence of the leader because such leader has built success around himself. Therefore, a leader who is charismatic must always be present with the employees to achieve success.

- **Democratic Leadership:** this is also referred to as participative leadership. Leaders who subscribe to this style involve their team members in decision-making, but they make the final decision. Employees of democratic leaders usually have a high level of satisfaction with their job, and they are often more productive. This leadership style helps leaders to motivate their teams to develop their skills. Employees believe they are in control of whatever happens to them. Therefore, the inspiration for hard and smart work does not come from the financial reward alone. Democratic leadership is not suitable for situations where decisions need to be made within a short period.

- **Laisses-Faire Leadership:** the French phrase "laissez-faire" means "leave it be." Leaders who use this style allow employees to work on their own without supervision. Many leaders resort to this style naturally when they don't have adequate control over their team members. These leaders allow team members to set deadlines for themselves but provide advice and resources, when demanded; otherwise, they stay aloof. This leadership style can be useful where the team members are skilled and disciplined enough; however, if the team members don't learn to manage their time well, they will not be able to meet their deadlines.
- **People-Oriented Leadership:** Leaders who use this style often emphasize the development of team members. They encourage teamwork and collaboration. These leaders are often approachable and friendly; they are

concerned about the welfare of all team members. With this style of leadership in use, every member is motivated and feel respected as a member of the team. However, leaders may take this too far that it begins to affect the productivity of the team.

- **Task-Oriented Leadership:** The only concern of leaders who practice this leadership style is the job to be done. They don't care about how their team members feel, they roll out instructions and expect that the guidelines will be followed to the letter and the job done efficiently. This style is fundamentally useful when team members are not disciplined with time. However, the team members will become disinterested in the work they are doing, and this can cause high employee turnover.

- **Transformational Leadership:** This style of leadership is best suited for business.

Transformational leaders motivate everyone on the team because they are optimistic about everyone including themselves. This makes the team members motivated to commit themselves more to the job, and the result will be increased productivity. However, transformational leaders don't usually pay attention to details, and this can be harmful to the team.

Discussed below are tips for creating a revolutionary culture for your organization.

- Have weekly meetings with your employees where people can open up on the challenges they are facing with their duties, and solutions can be provided. Also, inspire your managers and employees with daily inspirational quotes. They could be written in the office space or sent over the internet.
- Determine when to employ compassion-based coaching rather than compliance-based

coaching, and when to use compliance-based coaching. While it is true that you must care for your people, you must also achieve your set goals. It's essential that you study your people and know which will work for them.

- Encourage your employees to bring in beautiful ideas that could move the organization forward. This was Steve Jobs style; he hired people so they can teach him new ideas. Let your employees know that they can make suggestions and that their recommendations will be assessed objectively. Make the process for evaluating suggestions transparent, so that even if the idea is not implemented now, the employee will not feel bad and decide not to suggest an idea in the future.

- When an employee request for the opportunity to work from home, it should only be granted after you have assessed the employee. You need to know the reason for the application, the productivity of the employee in the past, the record of the employee concerning meeting deadlines among others. I don't suggest that you should not grant your employees the opportunity to work from home, because it has several benefits, like less distraction from colleagues, having more time to work because spending time in traffic has been avoided, among others. However, it can also make the employee not to work hard anymore and miss deadlines.

- You should also consider the use of analytics to help monitor your organizational data. Several organizations like Amazon, Facebook, Nissan Motor Company, among others all use analytics, and it strengthened the organization. Therefore, it can be an excellent tool for your organization.

CHAPTER SIX

BE INNOVATIVE

"Innovation distinguishes between a leader and a follower."

~Steve Jobs (Apple co-founder)

Steve Jobs is an example of an innovative leader. In the early seventies, he co-founded Apple computer with his partner. The startup was a hit within the first few years, but with the passage of time, and competition from other companies that produce personal computers, the Apple computer dropped popularity. Many people did not believe in Jobs' ideas because they were unique.

Jobs had to leave the organization later due to problems with products and leadership itches.

He moved on to creating his own company which later became the famous Pixar. However, due to his passion to make a difference, and his attitude of not giving up, Jobs returned to Apple as CEO in the nineties. On his return, he revitalized the organization. It cannot be argued today that Jobs created one of the biggest companies that make a significant difference in the tech world. Jobs is known for his passion for innovating, making a change, doing something new and motivating his employees. Steve Jobs was quoted to have said "sometimes when you innovate; you make mistakes. It is best to admit them quickly and get on with improving your other innovations."

One significant criterion for becoming a revolutionary leader is to be innovative. To be innovative is both to think and also to encourage others to generate novel and improved ideas so that the organization can gravitate towards increased productivity. Innovative leaders must be able to think differently than others, create something new using their thoughts, and also develop others to do the same.

Being innovative doesn't always mean that you are the one that generates all the great ideas, it could be as simple as recognizing a great idea even if a subordinate suggested it. The innovative leader also creates a path for bringing ideas into reality. Furthermore, the innovative leader communicates the concept to the employees effectively.

This is one of the reasons why I have always loved adding individuals to some of the teams I have led. I always encourage them to teach me great ideas on how to develop programs and seminars that are creative. I have experienced the benefits of having my team members lead projects while I only listen to and empower them. Today, some of the people who worked previously on my teams have become successful leaders.

In the present times, managers have to be innovative especially concerning the mental health of their employees. Recently, the NBA invested in taking care of the mental health of the players after some players made open confessions about their struggle with mental health. Innovative leaders should not wait till employees decide to speak up before they do something about the mental health of team members, there must be a system of keeping every employee in a good state of mental health.

Some of the characteristics of innovative leaders are discussed below.

Characteristics of Innovative Leaders

- **Innovative leaders listen:** Many people think of communication only concerning speaking. Therefore, they spend a lot of time developing their abilities to talk effectively with their team members. Just a few people learn to listen to others. To be innovative, leaders must learn to listen so that they can absorb and synthesize information from diverse sources. Poor listeners always misunderstand situations and messages being passed across to them. Good listening comprises of paying attention to what the speaker is saying, interpreting the message without preconceived notions or bias, asking questions to be sure you have understood correctly, and acting on what has been understood.

- **Innovative leaders are empathic:** Innovation is about knowing what consumers want and creating a way to meet those needs. If you are not empathic, there is no way you can understand what consumers want. In other words, it takes empathy to comprehend the emotions and motivations of human beings.

- **Innovative leaders are purposeful:** they are not usually in the business of aimless competition; they are always passionate about creating solutions to problems around them. They always seek to know why things are the way they are and what they can do to make things better.

- **Innovative leaders are observant:** anyone who cannot settle down to observe cannot be an innovative leader. They look, listen, comprehend, make connections, and observe some more. They take note of events, situations, behaviors and find out how they may be improved on.

- **Innovative leaders expose themselves to ideas:** ideas are the bedrock of innovation; therefore, innovative leaders seek out ideas. They read books, attend conferences, listen to other leaders to get new ideas. They are also very humble. Really, no proud person can expose themselves to ideas; they always believe that they know all.

- **Innovative leaders attempt new things:** The fear of trying to implement a new idea is what has kept many people from being creative. However, an innovative leader is that person that can take the risk of implementing a new idea and learn both from the success and failures of those ideas. Just like Thomas Edison who, after trying to get through with an experiment for several months but could not, said he has not failed, he has only learned new ways not to experiment.

It is worthy of note that people cannot be innovative where they are not experts. For instance, if a medical doctor who is not skilled in car designs is put in charge of a car company, he will most likely not be innovative because he is not experienced in that area. People who are trained engineers have more likelihood of being innovative when put in charge of a car company that those who are not trained engineers. This is not an excuse for any leader not to be innovative; there are myriads of opportunities that a leader can access to become creative.

Let us consider in details how leaders can become innovative.

How to Become Innovative

- **Look for problems:** Usually, innovation starts with recognizing issues rather than having a fantastic idea. Innovative people always look out for what others would call small problems before those small problems transmogrify into massive challenges that will be insurmountable. According to Steve Jobs, "when you first start off trying to solve a problem, the first solutions you come up with are very complex, and most people stop there. But if you keep going and live with the problem and peel more layers of the onion off, you can often time arrive at some exquisite and simple solutions. Most people just don't put in the time or energy to get there."

- **Take calculated risks:** I think you should know from the outset that not all creative ideas will eventually work out well. Yes, some of your ideas will fall flat; some of them will not yield the desired result. However, you should not allow fear to hold you back from trying. When you have considered an idea along with your team members, give it a trial, but keep an eye on the results. If it is positive, continue; if it is negative, be willing to change it immediately. There is no success in innovation without taking calculated risks. You must not fall into either of two extremes; the first extreme is to be afraid to take risks at all, and the other extreme is to take risks without critically considering what could be the outcome of the idea. In other words, to take risks arbitrarily. According to Bill Gates, "it's fine to celebrate success, but it is more important to heed the lessons of failure."

- **Inspire your team:** More often than not, you will need your team members in your journey to creativity. You must find ways of making your team willing and able to create new and better ways of doing things. It is often said that 'if you want to go fast, go alone. If you want to go far, go together." You will always need your team to see what you are seeing and to be as passionate about seeking a solution as you are. You must learn how to communicate passionately such that your team members will be inspired to become innovative like you are. According to Henry Ford, "coming together is a beginning, keeping together is progress. Working together is success."

- **Know when to jettison an idea:** One common temptation to leaders who are innovative is pride. They are aware that if they can successfully implement that idea, it will be to their honor. As such, they will do anything possible to see that the idea works. Sometimes, even after it has become crystal clear that implementing the idea is not the way forward, they want to find a way around it still. But true innovative leaders must let go of the ego so that they can stop an idea when it is evident that it will not work. When you are trying to implement an idea, and it's not working, there is no problem; just go back to the 'drawing board' and re-strategize. Confucius captures this well when he said, "when it is obvious that the goals cannot be reached, don't adjust the goals, adjust the action steps,"

Revolutionary leaders are innovative, break the barriers and come into the world of innovative leaders by paying attention to the steps discussed.

CHAPTER SEVEN

KEEP GROWING

"Leadership and learning are indispensable to each other."

~John Fitzgerald Kennedy

Irrespective of what your past looks like as a leader, you can take a deliberate step towards change and keep growing in that path till you begin to enjoy the rewards of leadership growth. I talked about Abraham Lincoln in this book as a great leader; you may be surprised to know that he wasn't always a great leader. History tells us that while he was a youth, Abraham Lincoln often endangered his future by being thoughtless. Also, he could not do well as an entrepreneur because he could not handle money properly. But at a point in his life, he started learning about the right way to lead, and he applied his heart to what he learned, and also committed himself to growth, he became a world re-known leader. What I am saying is that whatever the mistakes you have made in the past, you can still become a great leader in the future.

Frank Winfield Woolworth worked at a dry goods store before he created his Company – Foot Locker. The company (Foot Locker) became one of the biggest marketing chains in the world. However, history also revealed that when Woolworth worked at the dry goods store, his boss did not allow him to wait on customers because he was judged not to have enough common sense to meet the needs of the customers. Woolworth committed himself to leadership growth, and the effect was that his company prospered.

The journey to greatness is not a sudden flight; it is an accumulation of development in skill and attitude over time. No leader suddenly became a world acclaimed leader, everyone started small, and then grew over time. It is good to note that although time is necessary for growth, time does not automatically confer growth on an individual. For example, that a person has been occupying leadership positions for say 20 years does not mean the person is a great leader. You will find out in this chapter what you can do to grow as a leader. But first, let me give you some benefits of committing yourself to leadership growth.

Benefits of Commitment to Leadership Growth

- **Relevance:** Leaders who devote themselves to improving their leadership skills always remain relevant within the organization. Organizations experience change continually, if a leader is static, the services will soon be rejected. In some organizations that give promotion by performance, leaders who are not growing will not be promoted. So, to remain relevant in the scheme of things, leaders must develop.

- **Insight:** The ability of a leader to discover skill gaps within the team is increased with growth. In other words, as leaders grow, they can see more clearly the gaps that need to be filled within their organization for optimal performance. With this insight, they can decide to train the team members or bring in new team members with the requisite skills to join the team.

- **Productivity:** the organizations that employ leaders who are dedicated to growth will be ahead of organizations who don't concerning competing for customers. Leaders who are growing develop new and exciting ways of attending to their customers, packaging their products and hitting the market while those who are not growing stick to the method they have always used. To enjoy accentuated productivity, leaders must develop.

- **Development of team members:** one of the primary jobs of a leader is to develop other leaders. According to Ralph Nader, "the function of leadership is to produce more leaders, not more followers." However, for leaders to develop team members, the leaders themselves must be committed to growth.

Leaders are expected to lead by example, so, any leader who is not growing will have team members that are likely not increasing too. If you must help your team members to develop their skills, your skills must be growing also.

Let us consider in details what leaders can do to grow.

Tips for Leadership Growth

- **Write your goals:** Studies have shown that there is a higher likelihood of achieving your goals if you write them than when you don't. Never forget that your goals must be specific, measurable, attainable, realistic and time-bound. Also, remember that a goal is useless if it does not change your daily schedule. So, while you write your goals, also write your action plans – what you will do every day that will eventually culminate in the achievement of your goal. For example, if your goal is to develop the ability to speak with your authentic voice, reading a book on speaking on Monday, Wednesday and Friday, practicing to talk on Tuesday, and Thursday can be your action plans. You should also make your action plans SMART. So, you should specify the number of pages of the books to read, the amount of time to spend practicing to speak among other things.

- **Create space for leadership development in your daily schedule:** It doesn't have to be 1 or 2 hours, it could be as low as 5 to 10 minutes, but it is profitable to have a time specifically carved out to pursue leadership development every day. It has been said that the strength of great men lies in their daily schedule. Therefore, let your daily schedule reflect your desire for leadership growth and development.

- **Identify why you want to grow:** leadership growth is a lifelong process, and just like any other process that requires continual dedication, inconsistency, loss of motivation and zeal constitute a significant challenge for many people. This is why it is essential that you write your reason for pursuing leadership development. This is what will keep you going when the road gets rough. Many people, after reading a book like this, they will do everything suggested for 1 or 2 months, after which they will lose motivation and forget about leadership development. If you determine why you want to grow as a leader, you can keep your motivation and zeal for a longer time.

- **Allow feedback:** Create a system around you where your colleagues, team members, and customers can give you feedback about your leadership activities. This is critical to your growth as a leader. Learn to appreciate anyone who tells you what you are not doing right, and let them see that you are committed to change. Even if you don't agree with their submissions, never make anyone feel sorry for giving you feedback.

- **Be true to yourself:** what I mean by this is that you should tell yourself the truth. The journey to greatness is leadership requires hard work, if you must achieve this, you will need to go out of your comfort zone. From the onset, tell yourself this truth. Never believe the lie that things will always be rosy. You must keep a burning passion for leadership growth irrespective of the challenges you may face.

- **Invest in knowledge:** It is true that human wants are unlimited but resources to satisfy them are limited. However, if you desire to grow as a leader, you must invest your funds in acquiring knowledge. You will spend money to purchase leadership books, attend seminars, conferences, workshops, among others. I recommend that you assign a proportion of your income to leadership development.

Get a Coach: In addition to the tips I have discussed, you need a coach. First, for accountability, second for motivation. More often than not, when people quit in their pursuit of leadership development, they do so because they didn't have an accountability partner. An accountability partner is a person who will watch over your leadership development process. Such a person will be there to encourage you when you are down, check on you to know if you are doing your action plans, and also guide you based on his leadership experience. Due to the importance of the job of a coach in your leadership development journey, it will be counter-productive to select a coach arbitrarily. I will like to be your coach on this leadership journey. I have served in leadership roles and I have over 7 years of experience as a social worker. I have worked in challenging work environments and my colleagues have always described me as being a great listener, selfless team player, and skillful in being able to engage with colleagues with different and difficult personalities. Due to my background in social work, I am equipped to critically assess human behavior and work fatigue. This separates me from your typical executive coach.

Leadership development is critical for any leader who wants to be revolutionary, and I am willing to walk this path with you, to make your sail smoother. Welcome on board!

CONCLUSION

In this book, I have discussed the seven significant steps that will transform you from the leader you are at the moment to a revolutionary leader. You must 'look at the mirror,' reinvent yourself, diagnose organizational culture, be emotionally intelligent, create a revolutionary culture, be innovative and grow.

It is essential to note that reading this book is not enough, doing something about what you have learned is the main deal. I can help you with doing what you have read in this book.

Check my website http://mikempowers.com for more information. Or send me a mail through mike.empowers@gmail.com.

About the Author

Michael Appiah is a man who has always felt the allure of helping others. His passion to inspire and empower others shine in both his personal and professional life. He believes in empowering others to be innovative through unique ideas. Michael finds his leadership style is best conveyed by this simple quote, by Steve Jobs: It doesn't make sense to hire smart people and tell them what to do; we hire smart people, so they can tell us what to do.

Michael holds a master's degree of Social Work from Dalhousie University. With nearly a decade of experience in social work, he has been described by coworkers as a great listener, selfless team player, and having the ability to engage with the most difficult personalities.

When not fulfilling his responsibilities to the demands of his job, Michael dedicates his time toward helping new leaders become great leaders. He has spent countless years in various leadership roles, mostly through church/non-profit organizations. He even has a few awards to prove it. You can find out more about Michael by following him on his website, www.mikempowers.com.

During his free time Michael loves taking in a good basketball or hockey game. He is a talented singer and former member of the York University gospel choir. You can contact Michael by email: mike.empowers@gmail.com.

www.ingramcontent.com/pod-product-compliance
Lightning Source LLC
Chambersburg PA
CBHW030720220526
45463CB00005B/2129